☩Our Catholic Life

A READING AND STUDY GUIDE FOR ADULT FAITH FORMATION

1

☩ CREED ☩

THE HUMAN
JOURNEY
OF FAITH

Bill Huebsch

**TWENTY-THIRD
PUBLICATIONS**

twentythirdpublications.com

IMPRIMATUR

✝ Most Reverend Joseph R. Binzer
  Auxiliary Bishop
  Archdiocese of Cincinnati
  February 9, 2016

The *Imprimatur* ("Permission to
Publish") is a declaration that a
book or pamphlet is considered
to be free of doctrinal or moral
error. It is not implied that those
who have granted the *Imprimatur*
agree with the contents, opinions,
or statements expressed.

Scripture texts are from the *New Revised Standard Version Bible:
Catholic Edition*, copyright 1989, 1993, Division of Christian Education
of the National Council of the Churches of Christ in the United States
of America. Used by permission. All rights reserved.

TWENTY-THIRD PUBLICATIONS
1 Montauk Avenue, Suite 200, New London, CT 06320
(860) 437-3012 » (800) 321-0411 » www.twentythirdpublications.com

ISBN: 978-1-62785-173-2
Library of Congress Catalog Card Number: 2016939662
Printed in the U.S.A.

Contents

How to use this study guide in seven small-group sessions

Gather. As people arrive for each session, welcome them warmly and offer them refreshments. You may wish to have sacred music playing to set the tone. If people are new to each other, name tags can help break the ice. When everyone has arrived, gather your group and invite them to open their books to today's material.

Begin with *Lectio divina* prayer. Each session opens with a short and prayerful reflection on a scriptural text that is found in that section of the *Catechism*. Here are the steps:

1. Begin with the Sign of the Cross.

2. Read aloud the Introduction for this session.

3. Call everyone to prayer using these or similar words: Let us turn our hearts to Christ now and hear the word of the Lord.

4. Invite a member of the group to proclaim the Scripture we present for you.

5. Invite your group members to share about the text, first in twos and threes if you wish, and then as a whole group. Sharing: *What word or phrase in this reading catches your ear? What is God saying to us in this scriptural text?*

6. Now pray in these or similar words:
   O God, we know that you are with us and that you behold all we are about to do. Now grant that, by the power of the Holy Spirit, we might be faithful as we study our faith and charitable in how we treat each other. Through Christ, our Lord. Amen.

Read. Moving around the circle in your group and rotating readers, read aloud each numbered faith statement. Group members should note items in the material that strike them as especially important. Do not read aloud the **We Believe** statements. They are provided as an enhancement to the text.

Group or personal process. When you come to the process notes, pause to continue around the circle, discussing as the notes direct. Use our suggestions as a starting point, and add your own questions, prayers, or action plans.

Finish. As you conclude this session, call everyone to prayer once again. Reread the scriptural text we used in the beginning. Then move around the circle one last time to share: *In light of this reading and what we have learned today, what has touched you most deeply? What new insight of faith will you carry away from here? What new questions about faith have arisen for you? How will today's discussion work its way into your daily life?* Close your session with the prayer we provide, or lead a spontaneous prayer in which everyone shares their own prayer.

Session One

THE INBORN HUNGER FOR GOD

BASED ON ARTICLES 26-43 OF THE *CATECHISM OF THE CATHOLIC CHURCH*. TO READ A SUMMARY OF THIS SECTION, SEE *CATECHISM* ARTICLES 44-49

Introduction

When we begin to study what we Catholics believe, we don't start by talking about God. The *Catechism* begins by considering the human heart. In our hearts we find the longing that leads us to faith. In the human community we find the seeds of the Church. We come to know and see God in the world around us and the people in our lives. It turns out that we are religious beings by nature, and we find that we are made to live in communion with God. In fact, being with God is the only way to find happiness. So only when we listen to the message of creation and to the voice of conscience can we arrive at certainty about the existence of God.

Scripture

READER: A reading from Acts of the Apostles.

"From one ancestor [God] made all nations to inhabit the whole earth, and he allotted the times of their existence and the boundaries of the places where they would live, so that they would search for God and perhaps grope for him and find him—though indeed he is not far from each one of us. For 'In him we live and move and have our being'; as even some of your own poets have said,

'For we too are his offspring.'" (Acts 17:26–28)

READER: The word of the Lord.

ALL: Thanks be to God.

PART ONE + ARTICLES 26–28 OF THE *CATECHISM*

The inborn hunger

[1] The human heart is filled with hunger. No matter who we are or where we live, no matter how rich or poor we've become, no matter to whom we're married, or not married at all, no matter what, we hunger.

[2] And for what is it that we humans hunger? When we pause to consider this in all its magnitude and power, we realize that we hunger for that One who made us. We hunger for the divine heart. We hunger for God.

[3] This desire for God is written into our very hearts, because we are created by God and for God, and God never ceases to draw us to his own self.

[4] Only in God will we ever find the truth and happiness for which we never stop searching.

[5] Our dignity as humans rests above all on the fact that we are called to this "communion" with God. This invitation to be near to God, to talk with God, and to hear God's voice echo in our own souls is addressed to us from the first moment of being.

[6] The truth is that we believe something very profound about human life. We believe that we exist because God has created us. And God's creation, above and beyond everything else, is an expression of God's love for us and the world. Likewise, only through God's love do we continue in being.

[7] For us humans, we believe, it is necessary that we acknowledge God, acknowledge God's love, and give our very hearts over to God in order for us to achieve happiness and fullness of life.

WE BELIEVE

We humans are by nature and calling religious. We are connected to God and therefore we are fully human only when we live freely within this divine bond. We are made to live in communion with God.

[8] But how does this desire to be near to God play out in everyday life? How do we know that it is, in fact, a desire for God and not for something or someone else? In many ways throughout history down to the present day, people have expressed their innermost desires in words and actions. We have continually sought quiet moments of prayer. We have engaged in various forms of sacrifice. We have developed rituals and liturgies.

[9] We have found, in short, ways to express our inner being by reaching beyond ourselves to "another being." We give that "other being" a name, and that name is Holy One, Spirit Counselor, Wonder of Wonders, Father of All, Great Spirit, or, in a word, God.

[10] Looking even casually at history and how we humans have behaved, it is easy to see that we are "religious beings."

[11] And even though we have searched continually for God down through the centuries and even in our present day, God, it turns out, is really quite near to us. For in God, as Acts of the Apostles reminds us in chapter 17, verse 28, "we live and move and have our being."

Group or personal process

- When you think about your own life, how do you sense that you are on a "journey of faith"?

- What is your response to faith statement #5 above? How have you experienced this intimate closeness with God?

- Briefly share the story of your "faith journey," beginning with your birth and ending with the present situation of your life. Share about the people who introduced you to faith, taught you, were models of faith, and stood by you during major turning points that have occurred down through the years.

PART TWO + ARTICLES 29-32 OF THE CATECHISM
Knowing and seeing God

[12] God is divine love, and in Christ that love is revealed. Christ and the Father give us the Spirit of Love, and in this One God, these three Loving Persons form a perfect Trinity.

[13] God is very near to us, and we to God. God is as close as a breath, a smile, a turn of the head. And yet...we sometimes forget, or focus on the riches of this world, or allow indifference to overtake

us, or remain in ignorance about our deep desires, or follow bad example through sin, or ignore God's invitation, or even outrightly reject God, or—and this is perhaps the most insidious—*hide from God* in fear and shame.

[14] God, however, does not abandon us, or reject us, or shift the divine focus of attention. God is always calling us to seek the divine heart, to find life and happiness.

[15] And on our part, our human part, what is required of us? Simply that we open our hearts to God, that we allow ourselves to be loved, and that we open ourselves to hear the voice of the Holy One which never ceases echoing in our depths.

WE BELIEVE

We humans can arrive at certainty about the existence of God when we see his works around us in creation and when we listen to God's voice echo in the depths of our hearts.

[16] And for those who do seek God with a pure heart and deep desire, there are certain ways of coming to know the Divine Source of Life. There are ways of approaching God, of coming to see God, which make us rather certain of God's existence.

[17] We can't prove that God is there in the same way we prove something in science. But we can see with the inner eye, hear with the inner ear, and touch God in our own hearts. And in this, we can be certain: God is.

We see the world

[18] First, we can see the world. From the first glimmer of life, there was shining opulence in the midst of the chaos that surrounded the

earth. And as the Spirit hovered over that chaos, lo! Order emerged, *holy* order.

[19] However those first hundred thousand or hundred million years of earth's history unfolded, in all of it, we believe, the hand of God was present.

[20] St. Paul wrote of this in his Letter to the Romans where he said, in chapter 1, verses 19–20, "What can be known about God is plain to them, because God has shown it to them. Ever since the creation of the world his eternal power and divine nature, invisible though they are, have been understood and seen through the things he has made."

[21] And St. Augustine observes in one of his sermons that the beauty of the earth itself is a profession of faith.

We see ourselves

[22] Second, we know ourselves as human persons. We are open to truth and we see beauty. We have an inner sense of moral goodness. We experience human freedom and recognize the voice of our consciences.

[23] We long for the infinite, for the divine, and we question ourselves and each other about the nature of God. In all of this, we can see that we have an inner spirit, what is traditionally called a soul, that there is some element of human existence that draws us beyond ourselves, to our Maker.

[24] As the document *On the Church in the Modern World* from Vatican II puts it in article 18, we bear in ourselves "the seed of eternity." Indeed, that seed is planted by God's own hand.

[25] When we pause to let this seed of eternity grow, we find certain

knowledge of things divine. We know we did not bring ourselves into being, nor will we determine our final resting place.

[26] But even though there is that inner sense of the divine, and even though we are capable of knowing that God is present, we can only grow into divine intimacy by responding to God's invitation to this gift.

Group or personal process

- Share about an experience of "seeing God" as you observed creation: land, water, wind, forests, oceans, gardens, marketplaces full of food, sunsets or sunrises, mountains, animals, or, most importantly, your own beloved ones.

- In faith statement #23, we speak about having a soul that longs for God and draws us beyond ourselves. What is your experience of being drawn toward God?

- In Genesis, we read that we are made in the image of God. What does that mean for you? How do you see God in humans, and how do humans reveal God to you?

PART THREE + ARTICLES 33–43 OF THE CATECHISM
The Church teaches

[27] Indeed, the Church teaches what we have just observed, namely, that God can be known because of the created world and by the light of human reason.

[28] We humans are capable of knowing God, therefore, because we are created in the divine image. Even though we ourselves place obstacles in our own path to God, God shows us the way, provides us with signs and markers, and never leaves us. In order for us to follow these signs and understand these markers, we must keep our eyes focused, we must not allow other desires to overtake this one, and we must surrender ourselves to God.

[29] We are capable of believing only what we want to be true, rather than what is really true and revealed to us by God. This capability, this inner ability to turn away from God, even though God is Maker and Lover of us all, seems to reside in every human person. We are in need of God's ongoing revelation, God's sure hand to guide us.

WE BELIEVE

Despite our limited ability to describe God in human terms,
we humans can really name God. We ourselves are in God's image.
We desire that everyone in the human family should know God
as we do because without God we do not have human dignity.

How can we truly speak about God?

[30] The Church believes it is possible for us humans, of every religion and academic discipline, to speak with and about God. But our language is mere human language, so we look to what God has created to help us.

[31] There we find that all creation is a mirror of God; in a way, it reflects God's love and presence. This is especially true of us humans.

[32] But even under this method of speaking, our human language is insufficient and poor. For God is mystery: not a mystery of mis-

understanding or darkness but a mystery of depth, and we will never entirely probe the depths of God.

Group or personal process

- In your own journey of faith, how does the Church help you?

- How do your friends, family, or religious community help?

- In faith statement #28, we speak about our belief that we must surrender ourselves to God in order to find the pathway to happiness. In the mercy of God, we are able to find our way despite our own blindness and selfishness. What is your response to this?

- What other support do you feel you need in order to grow in your faith?

Prayer

We thank you, Jesus, for being among us here today as you promised us you would be. As we now leave this session, walk with us in our lives. Tenderly console our sorrows and heal our wounds. Keep our hearts centered on you, for you are the one we seek. Our hearts long to be near to yours. We pray in your name, for in you we live and move and have our being. Amen.

Session Two

BASED ON ARTICLES 142–175 OF THE *CATECHISM OF THE CATHOLIC CHURCH*. TO READ A SUMMARY OF THIS SECTION, SEE *CATECHISM* ARTICLES 176–184

Introduction

Now that we have considered the nature of the human heart and the longing for God that we all experience, it is time to turn to the question of faith. Personal faith is a giving of our whole being to God, who in turn gives himself back to us! This most amazing give-and-take, the to-and-fro communication between us and God, is only possible because we have the interior help of the Holy Spirit. Believing is a human act; it is conscious and free, and it corresponds to the dignity of the human person, which we just discussed. Believing is also a Church-related act; we don't believe alone, but we share our faith with others. Our belief is stronger because the Church guides us and teaches us.

Scripture

READER: A reading from the Gospel of John.

And the Word became flesh and lived among us, and we have seen his glory, the glory as of a father's only son, full of grace and truth. From his fullness we have all received, grace upon grace. The law indeed was given through Moses; grace and truth came through Jesus Christ. No one has ever seen God. It is God the only Son,

16

who is close to the Father's heart, who has made him known. (JOHN 1:14, 16–18)

READER: The word of the Lord.

ALL: Thanks be to God.

PART ONE ✛ **ARTICLES 142–152 OF THE** *CATECHISM*

Do you believe?

[1] "God," the *Constitution on Divine Revelation* tells us, "from the fullness of his love, addresses men and women as his friends, and lives among them in order to invite and receive them into his own company" (article #2).

[2] God, in other words, is a deep well of love and offers us the gift of divine friendship. God actually lives among us and invites us to be close to the divine heart.

[3] How do we respond to such an awesome invitation? What can we say for our part? Perhaps the only possible human response to such a divine offer is to allow ourselves to be wrapped in God's arms, as it were, to allow ourselves to be loved. Perhaps we can say to God with our poor human words, "O God, I do love you! I do desire you in the depths of my heart. I submit to your desires for me. I allow my whole being to love you in return. *I listen to your voice and I believe.*"

[4] We call this response to God by a name: we call it "Faith." If we can make such a response to God in faith, based on our deep trust in the divine offer of love, we would not be the first to do so.

17

[5] Abraham heard this divine voice and set out, trusting in what he had heard. Like us, he had no idea where he was going, or what he would find there, except that he did know—he *trusted*—that no matter what else, *God would stay with him.*

[6] Sarah, too, heard God's voice and trusted. From her trust flowed a great people, the people of trust, and the people of divine covenant.

WE BELIEVE

Faith is a personal decision in which we humans give our whole selves to God. We surrender our will and our mind to God. We believe in the person of God and in the truth that God has revealed to us.

---

[7] So when the Letter to the Hebrews defines faith, it reminds us that we cannot see God. "Faith," it says in chapter 11, verse 1, "is the assurance of things hoped for, the conviction of things not seen."

[8] And while the faith of the Old Testament is rich and deep, we have yet another wonderful divine gift. For we have been given the grace to believe in Jesus Christ. Furthermore, if we make a response in faith to Jesus Christ, God's only Son, we would, again, not be the first to do so.

[9] Mary, the mother of Jesus, believed before us and allowed her whole spirit to rejoice in God. When God spoke to Mary in the depths of her heart, through a divine messenger known to us as the angel Gabriel, Mary's response was clear: "Let it be with me according to your word."

[10] Throughout her life, in good times and in tough times, Mary

did not waver, and she always knew, as Abraham and Sarah knew, no matter what, *God would stay with her.*

In whom do we believe?

[11] We believe in God alone. We trust in God and in what God reveals to us through grace. We believe in Jesus Christ, God's Word made flesh, the one who dwells among us. And we believe in the Holy Spirit in whom we find strength, courage, and the insight of faith.

[12] Indeed, were it not for the Spirit, we ourselves could not believe in the first place. The Spirit reveals God to us, and only in God's Spirit can we give ourselves over, whole and entire, intellect, will, heart, and soul, in faith.

Group or personal process

*   When do you find it difficult to be open about your faith?

*   In faith statement #11, we speak of believing firmly and only in God: Father, Son, and Spirit. How do you make this key article of our faith part of your life?

*   How do you express your faith in situations where people are present who come from different faith traditions?

PART TWO + **ARTICLES 153–159 OF THE** *CATECHISM*

What is faith?

[13] Faith is a gift. Does that sound too simple? We just said a moment ago that, without the Holy Spirit, our eyes and ears would not

be open, our hearts would not be moved, and we would not be able to accept the truth.

[14] God offers faith as a free gift, and it is offered to all people everywhere and throughout all time.

Faith requires our response

[15] But even though faith is a gift and we cannot believe without the Spirit, nonetheless, we humans believe freely. We receive this gift only when we freely consent to it. Just as we learn to trust those in life whom we grow to love as our parents, friends, and spouses, so we freely trust in God.

[16] Faith, we would say, therefore, is a free act of our own as humans but in response to the divine invitation to be in relationship with God in the power of the Holy Spirit. Faith is not so much a response to what seems logical to us, as it is a response to God's own Self, as friend and lover, indeed, as Truth.

WE BELIEVE
Faith is a free and conscious act on our part. It is possible only because the Holy Spirit leads us to the waters of faith. We desire to live in faith.

[17] This isn't to say we are lacking evidence of God's love. In fact, in Jesus Christ the evidence is overwhelming! But it is to say that in response to that evidence, we give ourselves over entirely to faith.

[18] And this makes us sure. We are certain in our faith because of the long history of God's words, God's deeds, God's people, and *God's own Son*.

[19] We have within us a sort of "divine light" that gives us certainty unlike that from any other source. And under the influence of this divine light, we who believe seek always to understand more.

[20] Like those whom Jesus encountered in person, we want to see more clearly, we want to hear more completely, and we want to walk the way of holiness.

[21] The Holy Spirit helps us do this, helps us deepen and perfect our faith, by giving us insights, intuitions, sacred prompts, and deeper understanding.

[22] And because God is creator of all, and in Christ all things continue in being, and through the Spirit comes enlightenment, no aspect of science or human study is in conflict with faith.

[23] Indeed, by study and research and growth in understanding, we only come closer and closer to what God has done.

Group or personal process

- In your own words, how do you describe your faith?

- What is your response to faith statement #20? What do you want to see more clearly or hear more fully?

- How do you see the connection between faith and science? Do you see conflicts between them?

- What challenges to your faith are there in today's society, culture, or scientific community?

PART THREE + **ARTICLES 160–175 OF THE CATECHISM**
Believe freely

[24] No one is ever to be forced to believe. Indeed, because human freedom is required in order for faith to be genuine, how would such force ever be effective? We believe that in order for us to be made whole and to find perfect love in God, we must believe in Jesus Christ.

[25] It is up to us, therefore, to take care to nourish our faith, to help it grow and flourish through the word of God, through works of charity and justice, and through life in the Church, which is the community of faith.

WE BELIEVE

"No one can have God as Father who does not have the Church as Mother" (St. Cyprian, De unit. 6: PL4, 519). Believing draws us to the Church.

---

[26] In a real sense, we are already living in eternal life. Faith helps us peer into eternity and glimpse what eternal life is like. So we "walk by faith, not by sight," as St. Paul wrote to the people of Corinth in the first century.

[27] We live in a world which may seem far from love, a world over-whelmed sometimes by darkness. We see injustice everywhere, suffering, pain, sickness, and violence. But we must not let our faith be shaken! No matter what, as with Abraham and with Mary, *God will stay with us.*

[28] Even though faith is a personal act, it is not something done alone. We who believe share life in the Church and the community of faith in a centuries-long procession of believers.

[29] So, even though at baptism we say "I believe," when we complete our initiation at confirmation and Eucharist, it becomes "We believe." The Church forms us in faith through Scripture and Tradition as experienced through story, ritual, and symbol.

WE BELIEVE

Faith is necessary for salvation. It is a foretaste of heaven, and our faith is rooted in God's own self which he has revealed to us down through the ages and right into the present day.

[30] Liturgy especially forms us as God's people as we celebrate the sacraments, especially baptism and Eucharist. It is God alone who saves us, who lets us be what we are created to be, but it is in the context of the Church that we celebrate and realize this.

[31] In this sense, faith is essentially a shared act, and we give that a name. We call it "ecclesial." By ecclesial we mean "shared in the Church."

[32] And the Church, to help elaborate our initial faith, provides certain ways of declaring faith, or defining and understanding it. We give these ways of explaining faith a name as well, and that name is "doctrine."

[33] Through various doctrines the Church gives us a language with which we speak about faith. Down through the centuries, in dozens of languages, in hundreds of various cultures, people from every

nation have become the People of God and have held only one faith, have believed in harmony and unity, have celebrated one baptism, and have known one God.

[34] We now take our place in this People of God, in this Church, and we hold that same faith.

Group or personal process

- What makes faith easy for you to have? What makes it difficult?

- How does the Church help your faith? In what ways, if any, has the Church made faith a real challenge for you?

- In faith statement #29, we speak of shifting from a more private faith to a shared faith and we say, "We believe..." What is your experience of sharing faith with others in the Church? How has the Church helped sustain your faith?

- Who are the people in your life to whom you will also "pass on" this faith?

Prayer

God, the Father of Jesus, we would have no faith were it not that you love us so much. Only through that love can we see Jesus, and through your Spirit he is revealed to us. We cannot call him Lord without your inspiration. We pray now that you would increase our faith. Allow us to see and hear your word. Open our hearts and create in them a pathway to holiness that will end only in you. We pray through Christ, our Lord. Amen.

Session Three

MADE IN GOD'S IMAGE

···

BASED ON ARTICLES 325–349 AND 355–379 OF THE *CATECHISM OF THE CATHOLIC CHURCH.* **TO READ A SUMMARY OF THIS SECTION, SEE** *CATECHISM* **ARTICLES 350–354 AND 380–384**

Introduction

The faith that we hold leads us to believe that God acts among us in both "seen" and "unseen" ways. Using symbolic language, we often speak of angels as God's messengers and our protectors, even though they are unseen. We are created in God's image with tremendous human dignity. God willed the diversity of all the creatures and their own particular goodness, their interdependence, and their order. We experience all this as part of the "seen" world around us. God destined all material creatures for the good of the human race. We humans, though made of body and soul, are a unity of body and soul. We turn now to consider how this created order came to be.

Scripture

READER: A reading from the Letter to the Hebrews.

Now faith is the assurance of things hoped for, the conviction of things not seen. Indeed, by faith our ancestors received approval. By faith we understand that the worlds were prepared by the word of God, so that what is seen was made from things that are not visible. (**HEBREWS 11:1–3**)

READER: The word of the Lord.

ALL: Thanks be to God.

Visible and invisible

[1] The Creed we usually pray at Mass reminds us that God is creator of all that is "visible and invisible."

[2] When we speak of heaven, we must be careful not to consider it a place like the place you're in as you read this. We can't locate heaven anywhere geographically, or cosmologically speaking.

[3] We might call it a "spiritual place," because our feeble languages fail to find a better word. So, for example, when we pray "Our Father who art in Heaven," we're not referring to a physical location for God. God, of course, transcends what is physical.

[4] We humans have always had the profound sense that we are not alone. We experience the presence of other forces, giving us messages, protecting us, praising God as a chorus. We give this experience and these forces a name. We call them "angels."

Things invisible

[5] Our own sacred Scripture reveals to us that beings without bodies but with divine love do exist, and they are a great mystery. Who are they?

[6] First, we must remember that the images of angels that we have

in our fertile imaginations are not very accurate. Angels are purely spiritual. They really don't have wings and halos.

[7] They are, as we said above, divine servants and messengers, and we point to them as we do because down through the years people have repeatedly experienced them. Humans have always mysteriously experienced the power and ministry of God and named that experience the best way possible; we have named it angelic. The Scriptures are full of examples, and the liturgies and prayers of the Church reflect this ongoing spiritual experience.

WE BELIEVE

Angels are spiritual creatures who serve God. We venerate them because they speak for God and protect every human being.

---

[8] It was angels who protected Lot in Genesis, chapter 19; prevented Abraham from sacrificing Isaac in Genesis, chapter 22; assisted the prophet in Isaiah, chapter 6; and announced to Mary the conception of Jesus in Luke, chapter 1.

[9] St. Basil teaches that "beside each believer stands an angel as protector and shepherd leading him [or her] to life."

Things visible

[10] Using symbolic language, the story of creation in Genesis presents six days of divine "work" with divine "rest" on the final day.

[11] We understand from these texts that God created holy order within the world which reflects perfectly the holy order within the Trinity. So everything in creation reflects God and is a source for us to draw an understanding of the nature of God.

[12] Each and every creature has purpose, goodness, and divine origins. Each reflects God's own wisdom, God's love.

[13] Because of this, we humans must respect all that is created and avoid misuse of anything. This is a large statement today because so much of the world is polluted, exhausted, and turned ugly. We Christians are bound to develop an ecology based in Scripture.

Group or personal process

- In what ways have you been an angel to someone else? When did you act as an agent of God to touch, heal, or deliver a message of hope?

- And when have you received God's touch through someone who served as an angel for you?

- What is your response to faith statement #13? In what ways have you embraced this calling?

PART TWO **+ ARTICLES 340–349 AND 355–361 OF THE** *CATECHISM*
Partners for life

[14] And yet God made us all interdependent, each serving others and completing them. In a word, God made us partners with each other and the world, and with God's own self. The great diversity of creation adds to the order and beauty there, and all of it reflects the inner beauty of God. God loves everything and takes care of each.

[15] We humans are the summit of the Creator's "work," but there is

a solidarity among all creatures arising from the fact that all have the same Creator and are all ordered to his glory. In his famous Canticle of the Creatures, St. Francis celebrates the beauty and familial relationship of all created things. The text tells us that on the final day God "rested" as a way of blessing this day forever.

[16] For us Christians, however, a new creation is now unfolded because in Christ and his resurrection, we enter a new period of creative history in which God creates new hearts.

In God's image
[17] In the creation of us human beings, God allowed the divine image to be imprinted on our hearts and souls. Humans connect the spiritual and the material, the seen and the unseen, within themselves.

WE BELIEVE
God created everything to be good and gave the world great diversity linked to interdependence. All of us and every other creature is destined for the glory of God.

[18] Humans were created male and female, offered a role in God's ongoing creative impulse, and implanted with God's own heart, a heart for love. And this love extends as well between God and us. God our Creator also sustains us in divine love.

[19] And, while this can all be said about all creatures, it is said in a unique way about us humans, which is what the texts of Genesis reveal to us. For unlike other creatures, we are able to consciously know and love God in return, and we are called to share in God's own life.

[20] St. Catherine of Siena, possessed by love for God, once wrote

about this: "What made you establish [humans] in so great a dignity? Certainly the incalculable love by which you have looked on your creature in yourself! You are taken with love for her; for by love indeed you created her, by love you have given her a being capable of tasting your eternal Good."

Human dignity

[21] We humans are not merely another "thing"—created and lovely but only an object. We are much more! We are really *someone*!

[22] This gives us a dignity that is enormous, expressed in self-knowledge, self-possession, and the ability to donate ourselves in love to others.

[23] We are in covenant with God, responding in faith, which no other creature can consciously do. And we are, therefore, called to serve God, to love God, to seek to know God better.

[24] This all becomes clear in the life and ministry of Jesus Christ, the Word made flesh and the fullness of revelation. Jesus was a clear sign of God's endless love for us because Christ enjoys divine Sonship. He dedicated his life and death to restoring humans to wholeness in God.

[25] We can say, therefore, that all people share a common origin in God, all have been united by God's Spirit, and all are formed into a community by Jesus Christ in which we are sisters and brothers.

Group or personal process

- What role are we humans called to play in creation?

- Read faith statement #22 again. How is our human dignity connected to how we practice the art of self-giving love?

- What challenges do we face as citizens of the world in caring for creation?

- What do you see as your own personal role in caring for creation?

Two accounts

[26] There are two accounts of creation in the Book of Genesis, one following the other directly. The first is perhaps the more well-known because it is the seven-day story.

[27] But the second also helps us come to terms with who we are as human persons and how we relate to God. In it, we read the most amazing detail in chapter 2, verse 7. The author is retelling how human males were formed by God. "[T]hen the LORD God formed man from the dust of the ground, and breathed into his nostrils the breath of life; and man became a living being."

[28] With fantastic symbolic language, the author asserts that we humans are indeed of God's own breath.

[29] In ancient times and in the Bible, the word "soul" usually refers to the whole human person, but it can also mean "the innermost life of a person," a sort of spirit-within-us; it refers to God's presence, energy, and power within us.

[30] Likewise, our human body is animated by our soul, and we do not separate the two. There is an essential unity between body

and soul because both are created by God. God created our bodies and called them "good." We are obliged to honor our bodies, care for them, and care for those who live in material poverty and who, therefore, are cold, hungry, thirsty, or naked.

[31] In fact, this belief, that our bodies and souls are united as one, is so important to us Catholics that we include a physical aspect to our faith: sacraments, processions, corporal works of mercy, and work for justice and peace.

[32] We do not have two natures as humans, one spiritual and the other physical. We have one nature, called human nature.

WE BELIEVE

We humans were not created as solitary creatures. We are linked to one another as partners. The partnership of male and female is the first form of communion between persons.

-----

[33] God creates us entirely, body and soul united as one, in cooperation with our parents. We believe firmly in this unity because we know we are co-creators with God.

[34] We also speak of a person's "spirit," which helps us understand our spiritual life. And we also speak of a person's "heart," meaning the depths of one's being. Neither spirit nor heart introduces anything not already contained within our being, for we were created with an original holiness and inner unity.

[35] Men and women are created in perfect equality as human persons and they reflect the Creator's wisdom and goodness.

[36] In that second account of creation in Genesis, God provided

the male with a female companion, fulfilling a role that none of the plants or animals could. The male and female became partners, sharing humanity and love.

[37] Men and women are each other's helpmates, and, when they are joined in marriage, God unites them so they can have children, cooperating in the Creator's work. God also called men and women to care for the earth in the same way God would do that: with love, gentleness, responsibility, and generosity.

Group or personal process

- How do you honor and sustain the development of your spiritual life?

- Likewise, how do you honor and sustain the well-being or health of your body?

- What role does the heart play in your life of faith? In your daily life with your spouse or friends? And in the way you treat strangers, immigrants, or newcomers?

Prayer

Holy Spirit, source of love and faith, thank you for giving us eyes to see and ears to hear the word of God. We believe even though we have not seen. We trust in your promises and walk by faith. We believe that in faith all things can be done, and, like in Mark 9, with the father of the boy with an unclean spirit, we cry out, "I believe, help my unbelief!" We pray to you, Spirit, in the name of Jesus. Amen.

Session Four

THE HUMAN INCLINATION TO SIN

BASED ON ARTICLES 385–412 OF THE *CATECHISM OF THE CATHOLIC CHURCH*. TO READ A SUMMARY OF THIS SECTION, SEE *CATECHISM* ARTICLES 413–421

Introduction

Wouldn't it be wonderful if we all lived in the way that God intended and created us to live? But alas, it was not to be. With the very freedom that characterizes our lives, we turn against each other, God, and the earth itself in selfish and mean ways. We were created to live in paradise and be near to God, but from the beginning we humans have experienced within us an inclination to be self-taking and unilateral. This inclination is called "original sin." As a result of original sin, human nature is weakened and inclined to sin. Everyone except for Mary, the mother of Jesus, experiences this inner tendency toward darkness and sin. We now consider its origins and how the ministry of the Church addresses sin.

Scripture

READER: A reading from the Letter of St. Paul to the Romans.

Do you not know that if you present yourselves to anyone as obedient slaves, you are slaves of the one whom you obey, either of sin, which leads to death, or of obedience, which leads to righteousness? But thanks be to God that you, having once been slaves of sin, have become obedient from the heart to the form of teaching to which you were entrusted, and that you, having been set free from sin, have become slaves of righteousness. (ROMANS 6:16–18)

READER: The word of the Lord.

ALL: Thanks be to God.

PART ONE ✦ ARTICLES 385–389 OF THE CATECHISM

Created for paradise

[1] We humans were created good with the potential to live in deep connection with God, from whom flows all of life.

[2] We have the potential to love one another and to live in harmony with the rest of creation. One might say that we humans first lived in a state of "original holiness," sharing in the divine life.

[3] We can still glimpse this original holiness when we reach those moments of peace and when we pause to sense the divine presence around us.

WE BELIEVE

Revelation makes known to us the state of original holiness in which we were all created. We were born to live in paradise!

[4] We experience sometimes a sense of overall well-being, of absolute harmony: deep inner unity, love with our spouse or community, and peace with God.

[5] We humans were able to live as God desires and to be in control of our own senses. We were not subject to lust, greed, or lording it over others. It was paradise!

[6] The story in Genesis uses figurative language to describe what living as God desires is like: it's like living in a beautiful garden, having all our needs met, experiencing no pain or problems.

[7] What a pleasure it was for us to live with God as co-workers with him as the Creator! God, we might say, directed our hearts toward the goal of sharing divine perfection with himself.

[8] We humans, for our part, as is well known, did not achieve that goal. We missed the mark, as it were, and wandered into selfishness and sin.

The reality of evil

[9] One need not look any further than the daily newspaper to see that evil exists in our world. Who can escape it?

[10] And yet...Divine Love is infinitely good and holy. All of creation is good. So, where does evil come from?

[11] To fully understand sin, we must examine our relationship to God. For it is this relationship, based in love and harmony, that we reject in favor of our own futile desire. And what is our desire? It is to be *unilateral* (one-sided) rather than in relationship.

[12] On its bottom line, sin is an abuse of the freedom to love that God imparts to us all. Instead, we become selfish and unilateral: we use sex to satisfy our lust; we use money only to satisfy our greed; and we use others only to satisfy our dominance.

[13] We see only one side of life—*our side*—to the exclusion of the needs and desires of others, including God.

[14] Sin is not merely some psychological flaw, or merely a mistake, or the result of our upbringing, whatever that might have been. We do have such psychological flaws, indeed, but most are not sinful and many can be healed.

[15] We do make mistakes, no doubt about it. Not every mistake is a sin, of course. And for some people, emotional injury from family life does seem to set in motion destructive patterns.

[16] But sin is beyond all of this. It is an outright rejection of God who is love. In sin, we "miss the mark" of love, set for us by our Maker.

[17] In Christ, we see sin's opposite: we see a man who was unwilling to be unilateral and who called us all back to self-giving love.

[18] Christ reveals to us what sin is really all about because he sacrificed everything—everything, including his own life—rather than ever give up his love. In this, Christ the Son of God provides us with the grace to overcome sin ourselves and live in the divine light once again.

[19] All human beings are in need of this grace because all human beings miss the mark. We all wander away from self-giving love and toward self-taking thought and behavior. We all fail to love.

Group or personal process

- How do you experience evil as real?

- What is your response to the material in faith statements #15 and #16?

- Name the top ten evils present in today's world, as you see it. Then share what you believe our faith in Christ tells us about them.

PART TWO + **ARTICLES 390–401 OF THE** *CATECHISM*

The fall from grace

[20] The story of the human "fall from grace" is told in chapter 3 of Genesis. There the author uses figurative language to tell the story of an event in the early history of the human race. All the rest of history bears the mark of this event!

[21] We spoke earlier of our human experience of God. Sometimes we seem to hear a clear divine message sent to us through God's mysterious way of communicating. We give these wonderful divine messengers the name "angels."

[22] There is another force, however, that is more sinister and evil; it is also a part of human experience to sense a temptation to darkness, selfishness, and sin.

[23] God, we know, does not tempt us to sin; God is only goodness and light. And yet the temptations are clearly present.

[24] We give a name to this dark force from whom these temptations arise. We call that force "Satan." Satan is the origin of the force that makes us believe we can live without God, perhaps even prosper without God.

[25] It is a force that tempts us to think that being selfish and uni-

lateral is best, while being loving is for those who are weak. How foolish and how fruitless that is! Indeed, in Christ we learned that weakness is the way to love and the only way to human happiness.

[26] The influence of this dark satanic force has been and continues to be disastrous for the human race.

[27] But the good news is that there is a light that shines in this darkness and the darkness cannot overcome it, as John's gospel says in the opening verses. We humans have significant freedom flowing from God, which leads, if we are faithful to love, only to fulfill our destiny.

WE BELIEVE

God did not make death, nor does God delight in the death of his loved ones. Death results from selfishness and sin, from our revolt against God and the goodness of creation.

---

[28] But the choice must be ours. And only in the power of Christ and the Holy Spirit do we possess the spiritual energy or grace to make this loving choice. Christ, as it were, opened for us the gates to paradise once again, opened our hearts to the power of love, and set us on the path to divine life.

[29] Christ corrects our false impressions of God and invites us to live in the reign of God. And no one, especially not Satan, is more powerful than Christ.

Freedom put to the test
[30] We humans have freedom in God and this freedom requires us to recognize certain limits. There are certain laws found within

nature, for example, which we cannot break. The story of the tree of the knowledge of good and evil provides a figurative, symbolic way to explain this.

[31] According to this story, if we trust God and follow the divine way of life, all will be well; but when we are tempted to "go our own way," we fail. Tempted to be unilateral and self-taking, we choose badly and lose our original holiness.

[32] Then all harmony is lost; self-control is lost; mutual love between us is lost; harmony with creation is lost; eternal life in God is lost.

[33] It is not so much that "God punishes us" for missing this mark as that we ourselves choose to live without God, without love. And from that "first sin" came many more; the doorway to human misery was opened, and down through history the People of God have struggled to find their way back to union with divine light.

[34] Even in our own day, long after the resurrection and Christ's victory over sin, sadly, it still exists. One need only read the daily newspaper to see it, as we said above. Even though created as good and for good, we humans are drawn to darkness and create misery, death, and destruction.

Group or personal process

- In your own words describe the temptation to be selfish and unilateral. Where does it come from? What can overpower it?

- Read faith statement #27 again. What is this good news, and how do you experience it? How does love lead you to freedom and salvation?

Hope

[35] St. Paul in his Letter to the Romans helps us grasp an essential reality in all of this. All of us humans are implicated in sin but we are also all set free by Christ. St. Paul says it this way in Romans, chapter 5: "For just as by the one man's disobedience the many were made sinners, so by the one man's obedience the many will be made righteous."

[36] The Church has always taught that all people are born in love but also have freedom to reject that. It is, it seems, part of our original condition that we are *tempted* to reject God and *actually can choose* to oppose God's love.

[37] We Catholics baptize infants who have committed no personal sin in order to initiate them into the Church, the People of God, where grace abounds.

[38] There is great mystery in this for us, we must admit. God is good, and we were created in that goodness; and yet human nature was forever changed when our early ancestors rejected love.

[39] The Bible uses symbolic language, telling the story of Adam and Eve, to help us understand this. We give a name to this condition of being sinfully oriented. We call it "original sin."

[40] Here we use the word "sin" not to suggest a personal sin that we may have committed but a condition of life that we have inherited. It isn't merely that we humans copy one another by choosing to be selfish and unilateral but that we have within our very natures "the mark of Adam and Eve."

[41] Through baptism we receive the power to turn back to love, but the inclination to evil is not erased. Indeed, St. Paul wrote to the Romans, in chapter 7, verses 19 and 20: "For I do not do the good I want, but the evil I do not want is what I do. Now if I do what I do not want, it is no longer I that do it, but sin that dwells within me."

WE BELIEVE

Christ's victory over sin, selfishness, and death has given us greater blessings than those which sin took away from us.

---

[42] In the early years of the Church, there were those who believed and taught that human nature is not really deeply sinful and that, by free will and without God's grace, we could lead a good and holy life.

[43] Others believed and taught that original sin had perverted human nature and that, even though we were given grace, we were still no longer truly "good." In this thinking, grace was thought to have no power to change us interiorly.

[44] Both of these ways of thinking were wrong. We in the Church believe, in fact, that we do need grace to overcome sin and that this grace flows freely and lovingly through Christ. We believe that through grace we do grow in God's love. We also believe that this grace has the power to transform us and that, deep down, we humans are still good.

[45] And how do we experience this grace? It is experienced as a loving and divine energy; we experience God *empowering us* for love and life!

Life in the world

[46] The outcome of all this is that life is a struggle for most of us. We have a wounded nature, and we must admit that in order to overcome sin in today's world. The great *Constitution on the Church in the Modern World* from Vatican II helps us see the result of original sin.

[47] "The whole of human history," it says in article 37, "has been the story of our combat with the powers of evil, stretching, as our Lord tells us, from the very dawn of history until the last day.

[48] "Finding themselves in the battlefield, men and women have to struggle to do what is right, and it is at great cost to themselves, and aided by God's grace, that they succeed in achieving their own inner integrity."

WE BELIEVE

Christians believe that the world was created by God and is kept in being by God's love. Even though we have fallen into selfishness, which is apart from God's plan for us, we have been set free from it if we cooperate with grace. Christ is the light that no darkness can overwhelm.

---

[49] The really important thing to remember in this story is that, even though we humans missed the mark and our human nature was changed by it forever, *God did not change* his loving and forgiving divine nature.

[50] God remains loving and continually offers us the "good news" that we can return to him with our whole heart.

[51] Jesus offers us living water, gushing up like a fountain of eternal life! Indeed, the entire ministry of Jesus Christ was to set us free again! As St. Paul wrote, "Where sin increased, grace abounded all the more."

[52] And the Spirit empowers us to turn our hearts to Jesus and walk with him in our daily lives.

Group or personal process

- What is your own personal experience of original sin, of being drawn into the power of darkness?

- How are you helped by your relationship with Christ and your sisters and brothers in the Church to overcome it?

Prayer

Jesus, we are wounded and weak. We continually follow the pathway of darkness and selfishness. But by your grace we are forgiven of our sins and made whole again. Thank you for loving us when we are unlovable. Thank you for teaching us to cling to your grace and, through the ministry of your Church, to return to you again and again. We offer ourselves now as obedient to your will, and we pray in the power of the Holy Spirit, now and forever. Amen.

Session Five

MERCY, GRACE, AND SIN

BASED ON ARTICLES 1846–1869 OF THE *CATECHISM OF THE CATHOLIC CHURCH*. TO READ A SUMMARY OF THIS SECTION, SEE *CATECHISM* ARTICLES 1870–1876

Introduction

It's not really possible for us to learn about the human experience of faith unless we also take a deeper look at sin. Sin is an utterance, a deed, or a desire contrary to the eternal law. It rises up against God as contrary to the teachings of Christ. To deliberately choose (both knowing it and willing it) something gravely contrary to the divine law and to the ultimate purpose of human life is to commit a mortal sin. Venial sin is a moral disorder that is reparable by charity. The repetition of sins, even venial ones, causes us to be worn down by darkness and leads to more serious ruptures of our relationships with God and each other.

Scripture

READER: A reading from the First Letter of John.

If we say that we have fellowship with him while we are walking in darkness, we lie and do not do what is true; but if we walk in the light as he himself is in the light, we have fellowship with one another, and the blood of Jesus his Son cleanses us from all sin. If we say that we have no sin, we deceive ourselves, and the truth is not in us. If we confess our sins, he who is faithful and just will forgive us our sins and cleanse us from all unrighteousness. If we say that we have not sinned, we make him a liar, and his word is not in us. (1 JOHN 1:6-10)

READER: The word of the Lord.

ALL: Thanks be to God.

Mercy

[1] Much of the gospel and the works of Jesus concern the place of sin in our lives and the ways that we overcome it. Chapter fifteen of the Gospel of Luke sums this up for us by providing three of Jesus' parables.

[2] The first assures us that God seeks us; God wants us to "come home" just as the lost sheep comes home once it is found.

[3] The second assures us that God considers each of us of great importance—each and every one of us.

[4] The third assures us that God is waiting, like the father of the prodigal son, waiting for us to return, waiting to embrace us fully.

[5] All three of these parables portray God as, first and foremost, a God of mercy. God's love is unconditional and endless.

[6] For our part, what is needed is simple: to turn our hearts to Jesus Christ and to admit the times when we have missed the mark in order to take the first step and start the journey home.

[7] When we admit our failures like this, grace will abound for us. But grace cannot abound if we do not turn our hearts.

What is sin?

[8] The New Testament was written in Greek. When it speaks of sin, it uses a Greek word which is loaded with meaning: *hamartia*. This word means literally to "miss the mark," as when an archer uses a bent arrow and no matter how good the aim, the target is missed.

[9] It means to fail in one's purpose, to go wrong, or to sin. So when we define sin we must include this meaning, for we are created for a purpose; we are created with a target in life, and when we sin we miss that target.

[10] Sin shifts us away from genuine love for God and neighbor. As such, it goes against reason and nature and it also goes against right conscience.

[11] It wounds us deeply because it betrays our created purpose and it shatters our solidarity with our sisters and brothers in community. And as such, it is also an offense against God because God is Divine Love, and sin is the opposite of that: it is not love; it is selfish and unilateral.

WE BELIEVE

Sin is a deed or desire that flies in the face of God's intended purpose in creation. It goes against the plan of love in which God set the world in motion. It wounds us and breaks up our solidarity as a human family.

---

[12] For us Christians, the most intense lesson on sin comes during the passion of Jesus Christ. There on the cross, Jesus is in the midst of sin. There is murderous hatred. There is mockery and violence. There is cruelty beyond understanding. There is the betrayal of friends. There is abandonment by his closest companions.

47

[13] All so selfish. All so one-sided, so unilateral. In that moment, Jesus himself, suffering and near death, could have turned to curse his enemies, to join in the hatred, to reject those who fled from him, and to turn in on himself in pity.

[14] But instead, he clung to the love in his heart, nourished by faith in God who is Divine Love, flowing from him like a river, and he forgave his killers! He gave up his life, but he never gave up his love.

[15] It's unthinkable! But it's the way of Christ. He said to them, in essence, "Do you think this, *even this,* can stop me from loving you? Don't you realize that my love is inexhaustible? Don't you see that not even hate can overcome love?"

Group or personal process

- How does sin disrupt the relationships we share in our families, between spouses, in the Church, and in the wider social community?

- How do you respond to faith statements #12–14? This is the heart of the story for us. Read faith statement #15 again, and share your response to this good news.

- In your own words, share what your "created purpose in life" is. What is God calling you to be or to do?

How we sin

[16] It's a sad truth of human life, but there are many ways to sin, to miss the mark. Scripture provides several lists of them. See, for examples, Galatians 5:19–21; Romans 1:28–32; 1 Corinthians 6:9–10; Ephesians 5:3–5; Colossians 3:5–9; 1 Timothy 1:9–10; 2 Timothy 3:2–5. They include idolatry and sorcery, impurity, fornication, and lust, selfishness and greed, dishonesty, envy, and hatred, anger, strife, and jealousy, and many others.

[17] We can name sins by seeing which virtues they oppose either by excess or defect. We can name them according to the commandments which they violate or ignore. We can name them based on whether they concern God, neighbor, or oneself.

[18] They might be sins of thought, word, or deed. They might be the things we have done, or the things we have failed to do. It's a sad list, isn't it?

[19] In teaching about missing the mark like this, Jesus once said that sin comes from the heart, it comes from within us. But also within us are charity and grace, the source of goodness and blessing.

Mortal and venial sin
[20] We also evaluate the seriousness with which we miss the mark based on the weight of the sin. We have traditionally used two categories to describe the relative gravity of sin: mortal and venial.

[21] Mortal sin is deep and profound and relatively hard to commit. In mortal sin we turn our hearts away from God completely and

profoundly. In mortal sin we choose a way of living which is alien to love, charity, kindness, and joy.

[22] It isn't so much that we commit this single act or that which is mortal, but that we develop a way of living apart from God. We live in darkness and act that way.

WE BELIEVE

The root of sin is found in the human heart. When we freely choose to do something or fail to do something and thereby cause grave evil, it wounds us mortally. Such sins destroy love in our hearts, and without such love, eternal happiness is not possible.

---

[23] In venial sin, on the other hand, charity remains within our hearts even though we temporarily become selfish. Venial sins are those smaller actions or inactions that fill our lives day to day.

[24] But we must be careful and watchful: a pattern of regularly missing the mark, even though it may seem minor, if we are lenient with ourselves about it, can evolve into something more serious.

[25] We must remember that God is love and that we are created in that love. We are created only for love. When we miss the mark in a mortal way, when we move away from love, we attack our own very selves, hurting our very core. Because of that, the Church teaches that, when we are in mortal sin, we must make our way back to grace through the sacrament of reconciliation.

[26] As we said above, it isn't easy to live in mortal sin. Three conditions must be met in order for us to judge that our behavior or lack of it is truly mortally wounding to our relationship with God. First,

it must be a grave matter. Second, we must act with full knowledge. Third, we must give our free consent.

Group or personal process

- In your own words, what is mortal sin? What is venial sin?

- What are the gravest sins of modern life?

- In faith statement #25, we learn about how we sinners make our way back to the heart of God. What is your experience of doing this?

PART THREE ✛ **ARTICLES 1858–1869 OF THE** *CATECHISM*

Grave matter and free consent

[27] What is a grave matter? Well, simply put, some things are more serious than others. No one can make a list that is clear and certain, but we can say that certain actions "cross the line" from venial sin to mortal.

[28] Murder and hate. Adultery. Stealing, especially large amounts. Lying and slander. Defrauding others. Rape and other acts of violence. Greed. Ignoring the materially poor and rejected. Abortion. And others.

[29] What does it mean to have full knowledge and to give complete and free consent? It's hard to imagine not knowing that greed wounds us in serious ways, or that rape is a heinous act. But if we truly do not know that what we are doing or failing to do causes us

to sin mortally, then our personal responsibility for our actions is reduced.

[29] If we feign ignorance, or if we allow our hearts to grow hard, or if we permit a pattern of such living to evolve, then our personal responsibility for our actions is increased!

[30] The thing is this: we know that deep within us we hear a voice echoing in our depths that is the voice of God. That voice calls us to love and to do what is good and to avoid evil. It is written into our very core and conscience, so claiming that we cannot recognize serious evil is normally out of bounds.

[31] Likewise, we must give full consent to our decisions, freely choosing what we do. There may be psychological factors, or sociological ones, that prevent us from having full freedom, but we should be slow to blame others if the pattern of missing the mark is truly our own free choice.

WE BELIEVE

Repeating sins, even small ones, causes us to experience interior moral decline, preventing us from growing in faith and charity as we are meant to do.

---

[32] We pay so much attention to the patterns of sin and missing the mark in our lives for a reason. A good reason. When we die, the pattern of love which we have established is what we take with us into eternity.

[33] But likewise, the pattern of darkness, of being unloving and selfish, of being private and unilateral, is also something that continues into the rest of eternity. But even though we believe that certain acts

establish this pattern, we leave the final judgment about that to the mercy of God.

Capital sins

[34] There are certain attitudes and behaviors, named throughout our tradition, for which we must be especially watchful. They are often called "the seven deadly sins." These are ways of missing the mark that are at the core of what we have been discussing here.

[35] The capital sins include arrogance and boastful pride; greed and hoarding; envy and its accompanying resentment; hateful wrath; selfish lust; gluttony and ignoring the poor; and sloth or spiritual apathy.

[36] Finally, while sin is personal we are also sometimes complicit in the sinfulness of others. If we participate when others are doing evil, or if we order, advise, praise, or approve of them, or if we fail to disclose their evil, or if we fail to hinder them when we could, or if we protect them, we ourselves are also guilty.

[37] In all of this, we must always remember that God who is love has revealed that love in all its power through Jesus Christ and made us capable of love in return. The Spirit of love lives within us, even when we ourselves do not recognize or feel its energy.

Group or personal process

- What specific strategies can we Christians use to be able to see more clearly when we are blind to sin?

- In your own words, describe the capital sins and give some examples of how they challenge us in today's world.

- Our hope for salvation is found in faith statement #37 above. What hope does this belief bring you?

Prayer

Jesus, we turn our hearts to you now. We are filled with contrition, for we know we have acted with selfishness and failed to act with mercy and love. Our only hope is in your grace. Through the ministry of your Church, heal and guide us, strengthen and empower us, to become the loving men and women you have created us to be. We pray with fervent hope, in your name. Amen.

Session Six

BASED ON ARTICLES 1691–1709, 1716–1724, AND 1730–1742 OF THE *CATECHISM OF THE CATHOLIC CHURCH*. TO READ A SUMMARY OF THIS SECTION, SEE *CATECHISM* ARTICLES 1710–1715, 1725–1729, AND 1743–1748

Introduction

In this whole discussion about sin and grace, human freedom has been front and center. We are endowed with a spiritual soul, intellect, and free will. From our very conception, the human person is ordered to God and destined for eternal happiness. We are obliged to follow the moral law, which urges us "to do what is good and avoid what is evil." This law makes itself heard in our conscience. The Beatitudes take up and fulfill God's promises in Scripture by guiding us to live in the kingdom of heaven. They respond to the desire for happiness that God has placed in the human heart. We will learn here that the right to the exercise of freedom especially in religious and moral matters is an inalienable element of human dignity. However, the exercise of freedom does not entail the right to say or do anything one pleases.

Scripture

READER: A reading from the Gospel of Matthew.

Blessed are the poor in spirit, for theirs is the kingdom of heaven. Blessed are those who mourn, for they will be comforted. Blessed are the meek, for they will inherit the earth. Blessed are those who hunger and thirst for righteousness, for they will be filled. Blessed are the merciful, for they will receive mercy. Blessed are the pure in heart, for they will see God. Blessed are the peacemakers, for they will be called children of God. Blessed are those who are persecuted for righteousness' sake, for theirs is the kingdom of heaven. (MATTHEW 5:3–10)

READER: The word of the Lord.

ALL: Thanks be to God.

PART ONE + ARTICLES 1691–1698 OF THE *CATECHISM*

Human dignity

[1] In one of his sermons, St. Leo the Great summarizes our vocation. "Christian," he wrote, addressing all of us, "recognize your dignity and, now that you share in God's own nature, do not return to your former base condition by sinning.

[2] "Remember who is your head and of whose body you are a member. Never forget that you have been rescued from the power of darkness and brought into the light of the Kingdom of God."

[3] We believe that all humans everywhere on earth have great dignity and share in God's own nature. We are created, after all, in God's image, and God is love. We are, therefore, made for love, for a share in divine life.

[4] We are invited to live "within sight of God," to live as "children of the light." This means that we are empowered to put aside all the ways of living that are selfish, one-sided, or domineering.

[5] When we speak of "living with Christ" or of "putting on Christ like a garment," this is what we mean. We sometimes speak of "conforming our thoughts" to the words and actions of the gospel, that is, to Christ who reveals divine love to us.

[6] This is what we are made for; this is our destiny; this is our purpose in life: to enter into God's own heart and to love others as we do ourselves. The Spirit of Love is our guide and our empowerment. We are literally transformed interiorly by this Spirit, enlightened, strengthened, and made whole.

[7] Following the Spirit of Love leads to life. Anything else leads to death and a way of living that deadens our spirit.

[8] There is a line in the Book of Deuteronomy, one of the important "first five books" of the Old Testament, that presents this to us in a direct way: "I have set before you today life and prosperity, death and adversity."

[9] We are faced with choices like this every day, and how we make them, how we choose between them, makes all the difference. As we study our faith, the really important thing is to see the joy that comes only from obedience to God's way of life.

[10] When we are in the flow of God's intended purposes, in the flow of grace, in the flow of "life and prosperity," we live in joy and

peace, and with a sense of well-being. Even when illness comes along, or loss of property, or even violence against us, we know we are well if we remain in God's way.

[11] So we learn in our faith to follow the Spirit of Love, the "interior master of life," the one who inspires, guides, and strengthens us. We learn to recognize moments of grace that are God's actions within us. We learn to live the Beatitudes which Christ taught. They are a summary of God's pathway for which the human heart longs.

[12] We learn to see how we are missing the mark, admit that and be sorry for it, receive the endless divine forgiveness, and amend our lives to live differently.

[13] We learn to develop values and virtues to guide us almost like being on automatic pilot: we know deep inside what is right and just.

[14] We learn to live with charity for all, and charity above all. And we learn, finally, that we cannot walk God's pathway without the support of others, especially the community of the Church.

[15] And here is the key: all of this learning, all of this catechesis, is about knowing Jesus Christ. It is about walking with Christ in daily life, about putting on Christ like a garment. For Christ is divine love revealed in the flesh, and in Christ's love we find our real dignity. St. Paul sums this up in his lovely letter to the Philippians, in chapter 1 where he says, "To me, living is Christ..."

Group or personal process

- On the deep levels of human existence, what gives us dignity? How do we share that with the rest of creation?

- What makes you happy? How does the belief statement in faith statement #11 frame your happiness and make it possible?

- In practical terms, what does the fact that all humans share dignity mean for life on our planet?

- Make a list of those persons or groups whose dignity you feel is not respected. Now choose one person or group and resolve to begin the process of bringing dignity to their lives.

PART TWO + **ARTICLES 1699–1709 AND 1716–1724 OF THE *CATECHISM***

Human destiny

[16] By revealing God to us so fully, Christ at the very same time reveals our human dignity to us! Christ is, in fact, divine love revealed in our midst, and Christ has given us the Spirit of love to ennoble our lives with grace.

[17] The image of God is present in every person no matter who they are, what they believe, or how they live. Our destiny is to be with God forever. We humans actually participate in the light and power of the Spirit.

[18] We are capable of understanding life's meaning and of choosing the good with the help of the Holy Spirit. Deep within us we recognize the voice of God calling us to do what is good and avoid evil, calling us to love. This divine voice sounds in our hearts, and following this voice is what brings about human dignity.

[19] We live divided lives in a sense, on one hand wanting what is good, and on the other wanting what is selfish. We struggle between these two, between light and darkness. But Christ gives us the grace or power we need to follow God's pathway in our lives.

[20] When we follow Christ, his teachings and examples, we become a son or daughter of God, and this makes us capable of acting rightly, of choosing the good, of living for love.

WE BELIEVE

In the Beatitudes we are confronted by decisive choices concerning earthly possessions, power, and prestige. They purify our hearts and make them ready for life with God.

---

[21] And the pattern we establish while we are alive is the pattern we take with us after death into the rest of eternal life.

Blessed!

[22] What is the heart of Jesus' teaching? How do we learn what is right? Jesus took the teachings of the Old Testament and added to them his own divine wisdom. All of these teachings of Jesus are summed up for us in that brief canon of love called the "Beatitudes."

[23] In the Beatitudes we learn what it means to be blessed, to live as children of God. The poor in spirit will receive the kingdom; the mourners will find comfort; the meek will inherit the earth; the ones who seek justice will see it happen; the merciful will receive mercy in return; the pure in heart will see God; the peacemaker will be a child of God; the ones suffering for justice will see reward; and the ones hated for their faith will be glad and rejoice forever!

[24] Here in this little list we have a recipe for happiness and the map of the Christian journey. It sounds impossible! But we believe it is true.

Be happy!

[25] We all want to be happy, and this desire for joy comes from God alone. Only God can satisfy the longing of our human heart, only God who is love.

Living with Christ

[26] Why did God make us? God made us to know the divine heart, to love as the Spirit leads us to, and to serve in the manner of Christ, which is without limit. If we do this, we will inherit eternal life.

[27] Do you hear in this how the Triune God invites into the very life of the Trinity? God who is love, Christ in whom that love is revealed, and the Spirit of love, indeed! Such a way of living in happiness surpasses our human ability to understand.

[28] It is an entirely free gift of God, flowing from the energy of love, and it is grace, pure grace. The happiness we are promised, however, requires of us that we choose carefully what is right and just and good. This happiness is not found in wealth, or fame, or power, or human achievement. These all lead to false gods.

[29] No, the happiness promised is that of love alone. The pathway to that is God's pathway, and we walk it step by step through our everyday acts.

Group or personal process

- What does it mean to you to "be happy"?

- What is your personal experience of living by the Beatitudes? Which of them have you experienced?

PART THREE + **ARTICLES 1730–1742 OF THE *CATECHISM***

Human freedom

[30] Freedom is a much misunderstood term. We are created as free persons, but free for what? The freedom that flows from God and our created world is only a freedom to love.

[31] Yes, we may choose selfishness and moral evil, but we know that these lead only to being held captive by our passions. It does not make us free. It makes us into slaves. It is not how we are created.

[32] "Freedom is the power," the *Catechism* tells us in article 1731, "rooted in reason and will, to act or not to act, to do this or that, and so to perform deliberate actions on one's own responsibility."

[33] We shape our own lives by our free will. We can either grow and mature, following God's path to truth and goodness, or remain stuck in immaturity, clinging to false gods instead.

[34] The simple truth is that when we choose good over and over again, we become more and more free. As we said above, any other choice leads to living in bondage to selfishness, which leads nowhere.

[35] Of course, we must know what we are doing to be held accountable for our choices. If we are ignorant of what is good, or if things happen accidentally, or if we are living under the control of another, or in great fear, or operating out of sheer habit, or subject to a psychological condition that limits our freedom, we are not fully accountable.

[36] Likewise, sometimes we are simply exhausted and our actions are not entirely free, as in the case of a mother, for example, tending a sick child.

WE BELIEVE

God has given us the freedom and dignity of his sons and daughters, and we are free to seek him of our own accord. Freedom gives us the power to direct our hearts toward God.

[37] For us to be held accountable for an action or lack of action, we must *will it*, meaning choose it freely. We must foresee the damage and pain it will cause. We believe that the right to act freely, especially in moral and religious matters, must be provided for every human being and must be protected by government.

[38] We humans have our freedom, but we know that we do not always choose love. In fact, we have quite a long record of choosing to be selfish, of missing the mark of human possibility.

[39] From the beginning, it seems, we have made the choice of darkness. Freedom certainly does not mean we can "do whatever we please." This is a false sense of freedom because it is so unilateral, meaning it is "one-sided."

[40] We live in community, and we are made for love within that community. Certain norms and ways of living together in peace can be identified and named and we call these "laws." They are laws, but they lead to freedom.

WE BELIEVE

The right to exercise of freedom especially in religious and moral matters is an essential aspect of human dignity. It doesn't give us the right to say or do anything, but it does give us the freedom to follow our consciences.

---

[41] Christ gives us the grace we need through his dying and rising, and through his teachings and examples, to follow these laws. Failing to follow these laws leads us to being imprisoned within ourselves; it leads to disrupting neighborly relationships; and it leads to detachment from God.

[42] This grace of Christ is powerful enough for anything we need. It leads us to discover the sense of truth, the strong sense of good, which God places in our hearts. The more we follow the inner prompting of grace, the life of the Spirit within us, the freer we become. And the freer we become, the more ready we are to collaborate with the Holy Spirit in God's work in the Church and the world.

Group or personal process

- Living in a democratic society poses many challenges to the concept of freedom. What is freedom, in your own words?

- How do you experience the grace described in faith statements #41 and #42?

- How do you understand the role of law in your life—civil and criminal law as well as the law of the Church?

Prayer

Lord, you have blessed us with the spiritual insights that make us persons of your kingdom. We desire to be poor in spirit, to be humble, meek, and merciful. We hope for peace and justice. You have made us wonderfully full of desire to live as your sons and daughters. Now grant us the grace to fulfill this great calling and transform our lives to do your will. Amen.

Session Seven

THE COMMUNION OF SAINTS AND THE END OF LIFE

BASED ON ARTICLES 946–959, 963–972, 976–983, 988–1014, & 1020–1050 OF THE *CATECHISM OF THE CATHOLIC CHURCH*. TO READ A SUMMARY OF THIS SECTION, SEE *CATECHISM* ARTICLES 960–962, 973–975, 984–987, 1015–1019, AND 1051–1060

Introduction

Given all we have learned about the human heart, the mercy of God, the reality of sin, and human freedom, one thing stands out as truly necessary: belonging to the Church. We as Church are a communion of saints united above all by the Eucharist. Everyone receives his or her eternal recompense from the moment of his or her death in a particular judgment by Christ, the judge of the living and the dead. By virtue of the communion of saints, the Church commends the dead to God's mercy and offers her prayers, especially the holy sacrifice of the Eucharist, on their behalf. Let us turn our attention now to consider what happens at the end of life, how we are judged, and how the patterns of our lives now lead us to eternal life.

Scripture

READER: A reading from the Letter of Paul to the Corinthians.

Now if Christ is proclaimed as raised from the dead, how can some of you say there is no resurrection of the dead? If there is no resurrection of the dead, then Christ has not been raised; and if Christ has not been raised, then our proclamation has been in vain and your faith has been in vain. (1 CORINTHIANS 15:12–14)

READER: The word of the Lord.

ALL: Thanks be to God.

The communion of saints

[1] The Church is the communion of saints, and the communion of saints is the Church. What does this mean?

[2] The Acts of the Apostles paints a picture of life in the early Christian community. In the second chapter, the author is describing how those who received Peter's first preaching responded. Peter was very enthusiastic because he had seen the risen Lord and later received the Holy Spirit at Pentecost. "So those who welcomed his message were baptized," Acts says in chapter 2, verse 41, "and that day about three thousand persons were added."

[3] "They devoted themselves to the apostles' teaching and fellowship," Acts goes on, "to the breaking of bread and the prayers."

[4] Acts is here describing the community of the Church, a community of faith. It is also a community of sacraments, especially of the Eucharist. It is also a community of gifts from the Spirit, of shared property and money, and of charity. This community, the earliest form of Church, is the communion of saints.

[5] Those who have gone before us, marked with the sign of faith, remain with us in this communion of saints. Likewise, those who are presently members of the Church around us are part of this holy communion. And, likewise, those whom we believe are being purified after death in order to be ready for eternal life join with us in this communion.

WE BELIEVE

The Church is a communion of saints. We are the body of Christ and we gather as a holy people. We draw close to Christ and share in his paschal mystery. It is dying to ourselves— with, in, and through Christ—that makes us holy.

---

[6] The saints, among whom we ourselves are numbered, bring us solace, support, example, and faith. And for this reason, we Christians have always honored our dead and prayed with them.

Forgiveness of sins

[7] We believe in the forgiveness of sins for the saints and for ourselves, which we profess in the Apostles' Creed. We believe that God is endlessly forgiving.

[8] For us Christians, baptism is essential because it is the first and foremost sacrament of the forgiveness of sins. It unites us with Christ, who is God's love revealed. In his death and resurrection Christ brings us new life with him.

[9] But baptism is not the end of the story. We must continue to grow in self-giving love. For even though we are baptized and have died in Christ, we are not set free from our inclination to sin, to

being selfish, to acting unilaterally, or to living in darkness.

[10] Who is strong enough to overcome this inclination each and every time it presents itself? Only Mary, Jesus' mother, and Jesus himself.

[11] For the rest of us, the Church holds the key: it is the sacrament of reconciliation through which we can reconcile ourselves to the gospel over and over again. In this sacrament, this sign of love, it is Christ who acts, not the priest or the Church.

[12] Christ is the Incarnate Son of God, and throughout his ministry among us, he worked to reconcile us with divine love, which is the only truth we know. Being reconciled like this—admitting how we've failed to love and receiving grace to amend our lives—is the secret to the reign of God. The apostles were given this secret, this "key to the kingdom."

[13] Now in our own day, standing in the place of Christ as a sign, the Church through her ministry offers each of us this same reconciliation in the power of the Spirit of love.

[14] There is no offense, no matter how great, that Christ through the Church will not forgive, according to article 982 of the *Catechism*.

[15] For divine love is unconditional; it is a "given-ness before" we act or fail to act in ways that "miss the mark." Forgiveness is given-ness before: it is unconditional love.

Group or personal process

• Share about one or two people who have died but who are still present to you in powerful ways. These people are in your communion of saints.

- What hope do you take from faith statement #14? God's forgiveness is endless and his mercy is forever!

- Being conscious of God's endless forgiveness and mercy toward us is what makes us forgiving and merciful toward others. Over the course of your life, how have you experienced this divine mercy? How have you offered mercy in turn to others?

PART TWO +

ARTICLES 988–1014 AND 1020–1027 OF THE *CATECHISM*

Our own resurrection

[16] One of the great Christian mysteries is belief in the resurrection of the dead. We profess this belief in both creeds, the Apostles' and the Nicene. Indeed, this belief has been part of Christian faith from the very earliest years. But what does it mean?

[17] The ancient people of God—Abraham, Sarah, Moses, and others—probably did not believe in resurrection. But slowly it dawned on the People of the Covenant that we live in eternal divine love and will share forever in eternal life.

[18] The Pharisees and other contemporaries of Christ did believe in resurrection and Christ himself teaches it firmly. Indeed, Jesus says that he is *"the resurrection and the life..."* It is Christ, then, who will raise us up as well.

[19] Encounters with the risen Christ are the foundation of our faith. It is, indeed, a great mystery; beyond the immortal soul, we believe our mortal bodies will rise to new life.

[20] After death, we believe, our bodies do decay while we ourselves in our essence remain in the power of God. How? Like a grain of wheat that goes into the ground and must die in itself in order for a new plant to grow, so we are but a kernel and will be raised with eternal power.

WE BELIEVE

All who die in Christ's grace are the People of God beyond death.
We may be purified for a while, but we will share eternal life with God.

---

[21] Eternal life has no beginning and no end, and we are therefore already on our eternal pathway. Indeed, we already share in the resurrection and ongoing presence of the Spirit of love.

[22] Each time we celebrate Eucharist we celebrate this mysterious reality. Christ is present. Love is revealed. The Spirit of love surrounds us. Amen.

Death

[23] Death is the end of earthly life. The clock ticks on and measures our lives. In due course, we change, we grow old, and in time, we die. This lends certain urgency to our lives: we have only a limited time to fulfill our destiny.

[24] We Christians understand death to be a vital part of life! In a sense, we haven't really lived until we've died! Why? Because we live in Christ who is love and when we die, the love we have in our heart is what we take with us.

[25] That love is also what we leave behind. So if we live in Christ we also die in that same Christ and live in divine love forever. There is simply no greater way to live or die!

Life everlasting

[26] As we suggested above, there is a judgment that occurs at the time of our death. This is not a judgment, however, like those in a court room in modern culture. Rather, how we have lived is reflected in a more loving way in an eternal mirror.

[27] St. John of the Cross put it simply when he wrote, "At the evening of life, we shall be judged on our love." Heaven is that fullness of life which is eternal, where we live in perpetual friendship with God, shared with the communion of saints.

[28] It is the deepest longing of every human to live in love, because we were made for love from the beginning—and for nothing else!

[29] St. Ambrose put this extremely well when he wrote, "For life is to be with Christ; where Christ is, there is life, there is the kingdom." This is all a great mystery, not a mystery of misunderstanding or confusion, but one of depth. How can we probe the divine depths?

[30] Indeed, St. Paul wrote to the Corinthians about this. This is in the First Letter to the Corinthians, chapter 2, verse 9, but Paul is quoting Isaiah, chapter 64, verse 4. "No eye has seen, nor ear heard," he wrote, "nor the human heart conceived, what God has prepared for those who love..." Indeed, "for those who love" with divine love.

Group or personal process

• How do you understand what happens to us at death?

• How do you respond to faith statement #28 above? Why does this give us such hope?

- Meditate on the last sentence of the Hail Mary. What do these words mean to you?

- Do you fear death? Do you look forward to it with happy anticipation?

- What do you expect to take with you into the rest of eternity after you die?

PART THREE +

ARTICLES 1028–1050 AND 1061–1065 OF THE CATECHISM

Being cleansed

[31] Purgatory is the name we give to that process by which we believe that those who die in "imperfect love" are purified. It is an expression of our belief that God is eternally forgiving and good.

[32] We honor and pray for the dead especially at the Eucharist because we connect our understanding of Eucharist with the communion of saints. We are one continuous family of God, and by offering ourselves to each other in love, love abounds!

Hell

[33] Hell is always something we choose for ourselves. When we reject God by rejecting love, we live in hate and selfishness. This is what we mean by living in hell. It is the hell that we choose for ourselves, not one that God thrusts upon us.

[34] Christ provides a rather disturbing picture of this in Matthew, chapter 25. In Matthew's gospel, it is significant that this passage

occurs as the final teaching before Jesus begins his "way of the cross." In fact, this teaching shows us our own "way of the cross."

WE BELIEVE

The Church prays that no one should be lost. We place our hope in God that all may be saved, and we believe that in him, all things are possible.

[35] In our tradition, we have come to understand that whoever does not live in love lives in death and has no eternal life in him or her. So here in Matthew, Christ teaches that if we fail to meet the needs of the poor, we thereby separate ourselves from divine love.

[36] That separation is hell no matter how comfortable we may seem now. When we make this a freely chosen pattern in life, a pattern of rejecting love, we make a definitive choice to live in hell.

[37] To die without seeing this and changing is to condemn oneself to an eternity without the presence of God, who is love. Again, it is important to note that God, who is eternal love, sends no one to hell. We must be watchful during our lives, trust the guiding hand of the Church, and reconcile ourselves over and over in order to be certain we are saved from this final damnation!

The Last Judgment

[38] What we have to say about the Last Judgment has, in a sense, already been said above. In the powerful presence of Christ, who is love revealed, who is truth itself, the patterns of our lives, whether loving or hating, will be laid bare.

[39] Indeed, this will be a glorious day! Love is stronger than hate. Life is stronger than death. Light is stronger than darkness. As

John the Baptist called everyone "to prepare the way of the Lord," so this final day of judgment calls on us to live in preparation for eternal life.

[40] For we believe that the kingdom of God will one day be fully established among us. Humanity will be transformed in divine love, and we will live on a "new earth."

[41] Slowly, progressively, the human family is prepared so that ultimately love will reign and darkness will be driven out. It's not easy to believe this because darkness seems to overwhelm us sometimes. But Christ is the light that shines in the darkness and which the darkness cannot overcome.

[42] Love is stronger than hate. Life is stronger than death. Light is stronger than darkness. We believe that every tear will be wiped away and all the just will be transformed, along with the earth itself, into the full reign of God.

[43] This great hope may seem foolish to those of no faith, but to us who believe, we experience a taste of it each time we celebrate Eucharist, each time we choose love over hate, each time we share what we have, or visit the sick, or give food to the hungry. This hope is the reason we care for the earth, fight against injustice, and seek peace with all our strength.

Group or personal process

- In your own words, based on your understanding of Church teachings, describe heaven, purgatory, and hell as you would to someone new to the faith.

- Why is the belief stated in faith statement #43 so important to our faith?

Prayer

Jesus, with faith in you and the witness of the apostles, we do believe in the resurrection of the body and life everlasting. We believe that, by virtue of our baptism, we now live with your grace. With the prophets and St. Paul, we proclaim that no eye has seen, nor ear heard, nor the human heart conceived, what you have prepared for those who love. We pray with grateful hearts for this wonderful gift. Amen.